BOOK 3

Current Hits for Teens

6 Graded Selections for Late Intermediate Pianists

Arranged by Dan Coates

Teenage students love being able to play popular pieces by their favorite recording artists or from blockbuster movies and TV shows. This collection includes accessible arrangements of pop and movie hits from Owl City, Alex Clare, Bruno Mars and many more! The arrangements are "teacher friendly," while remaining faithful to the sound of the original recording. In this late-intermediate collection, rhythmic difficulty is increased, and key-signatures include up to three flats or two sharps.

Produced by
Alfred Music
P.O. Box 10003
Van Nuys, CA 91410-0003
alfred.com

Printed in USA.

ISBN-10: 0-7390-9837-3
ISBN-13: 978-0-7390-9837-0

Cover Images
A piano keyboard waves on white: © shutterstock.com / Dr. Cloud •
stage with light and smoke background: © shutterstock.com / Filipe B. Varela

get._____ But be - tween the drinks and sub - tle things, the holes in my a - pol - o - gies, I'm try - ing hard to take it back. So if by the time_____the bar clos - es and you feel like fall - ing down, I'll car - ry you home. To - night_____ we are young._____

mf

So let's set the world on fi - re, we can burn bright - er_____ than the sun.

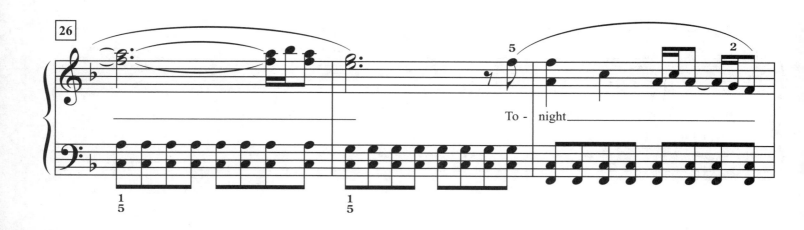

To - night_____

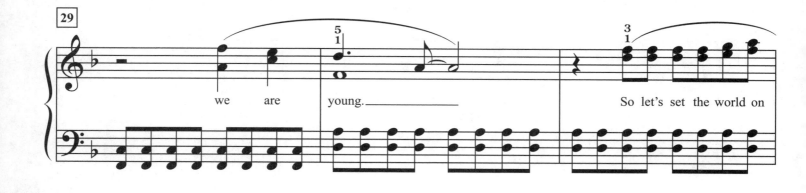

we are young._____ So let's set the world on

to Coda ⊕

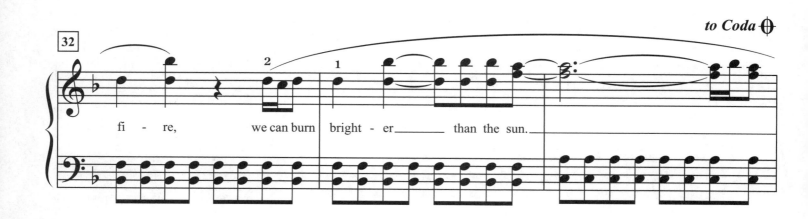

fi - re, we can burn bright - er_____ than the sun._____

17

PAYPHONE

Words and Music by WIZ KHALIFA, ADAM LEVINE,
BENJAMIN LEVIN, AMMAR MALIK,
JOHAN SCHUSTER and DANIEL OMELIO
Arranged by Dan Coates

11

It's e - ven hard - er to pic - ture that you're not here next to me.
I gave you my love to bor - row, but you just gave it a - way.

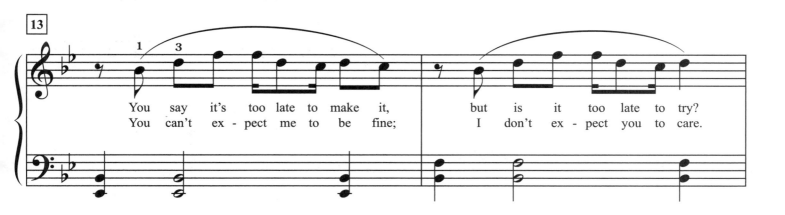

13

You say it's too late to make it, but is it too late to try?
You can't ex - pect me to be fine; I don't ex - pect you to care.

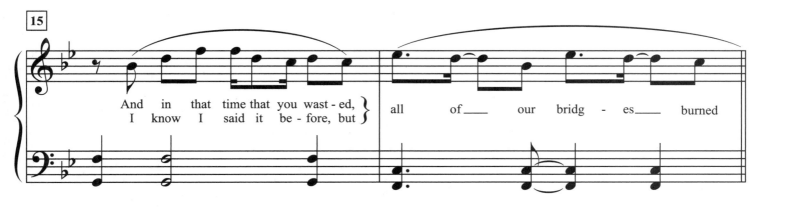

15

And in that time that you wast - ed, all of___ our bridg - es___ burned
I know I said it be - fore, but

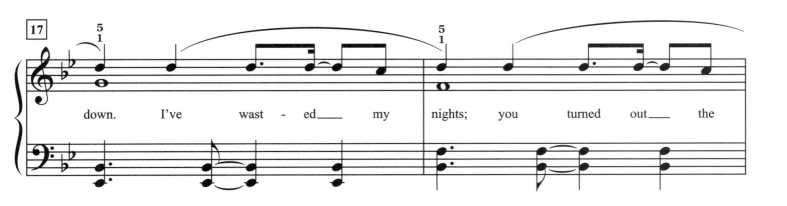

17

down. I've wast - ed___ my nights; you turned out___ the

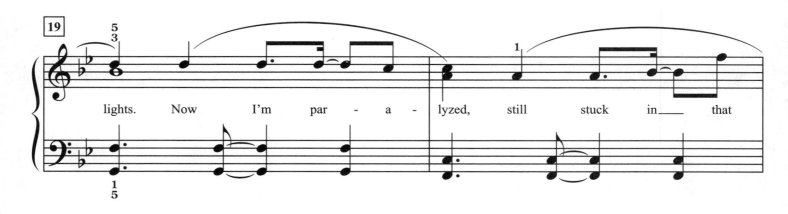

lights. Now I'm par - a - lyzed, still stuck in____ that

time when we called____ it love. But e - ven____ the

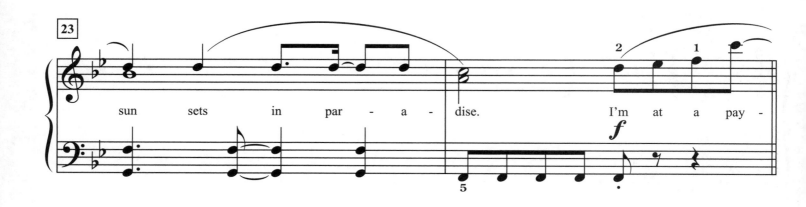

sun sets in par - a - dise. I'm at a pay -

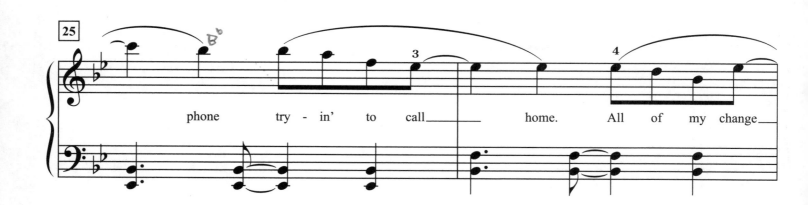

phone try - in' to call____ home. All of my change____

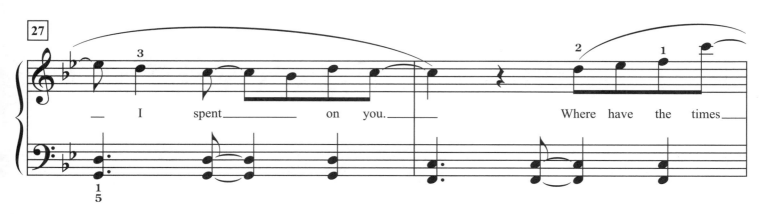

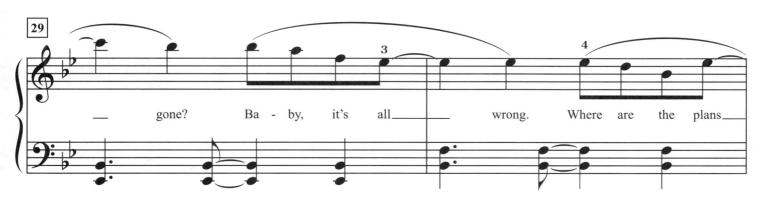

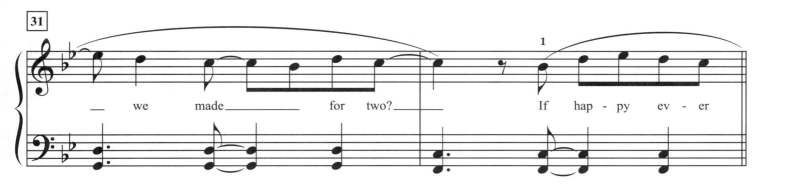

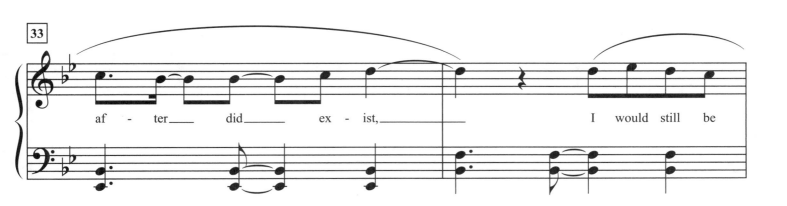

hold - ing___ you___ like this.___ All those fair - y

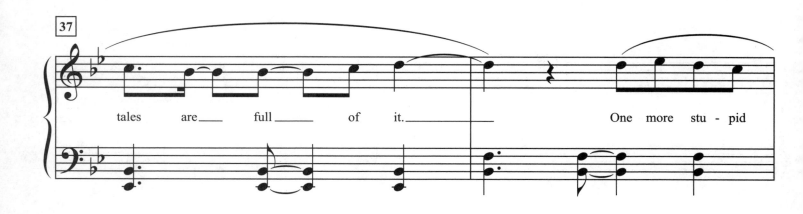

tales are___ full___ of it.___ One more stu - pid

1.

love song I'll___ be sick.___ Oh.___

2.

love song I'll___ be sick.___ Now I'm at a pay - phone.___

WHEN I WAS YOUR MAN

Words and Music by PHILIP LAWRENCE,
ANDREW WYATT, BRUNO MARS and ARI LEVINE
Arranged by Dan Coates

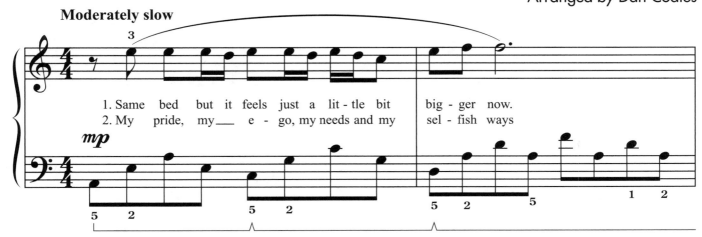

1. Same bed but it feels just a lit-tle bit big-ger now.
2. My pride, my e - go, my needs and my sel - fish ways

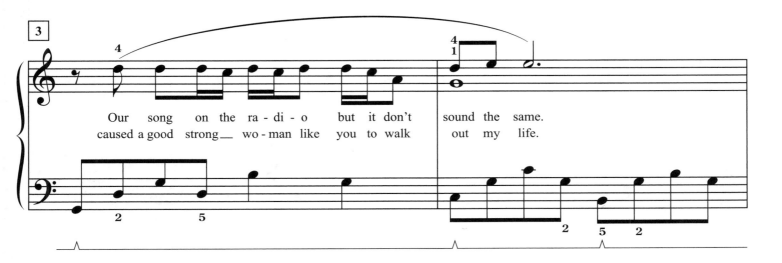

Our song on the ra - di - o but it don't sound the same.
caused a good strong wo - man like you to walk out my life.

When our friends talk a - bout you all it does is just tear me down,
Now I nev - er, nev - er get to clean up the mess I made,

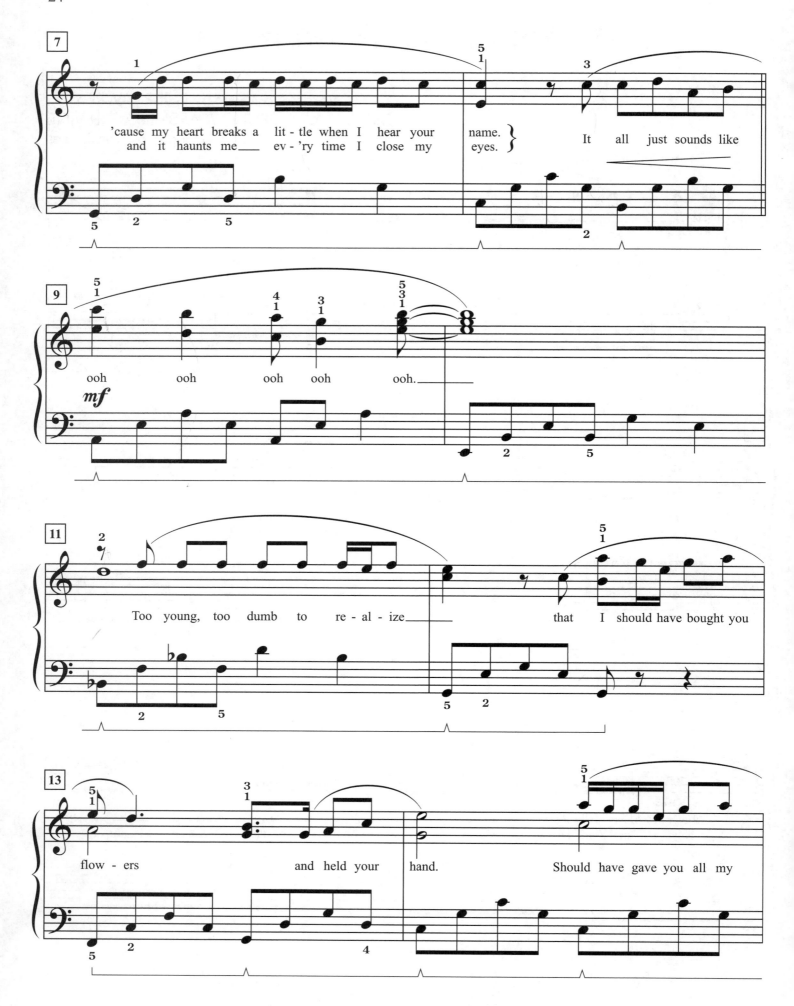

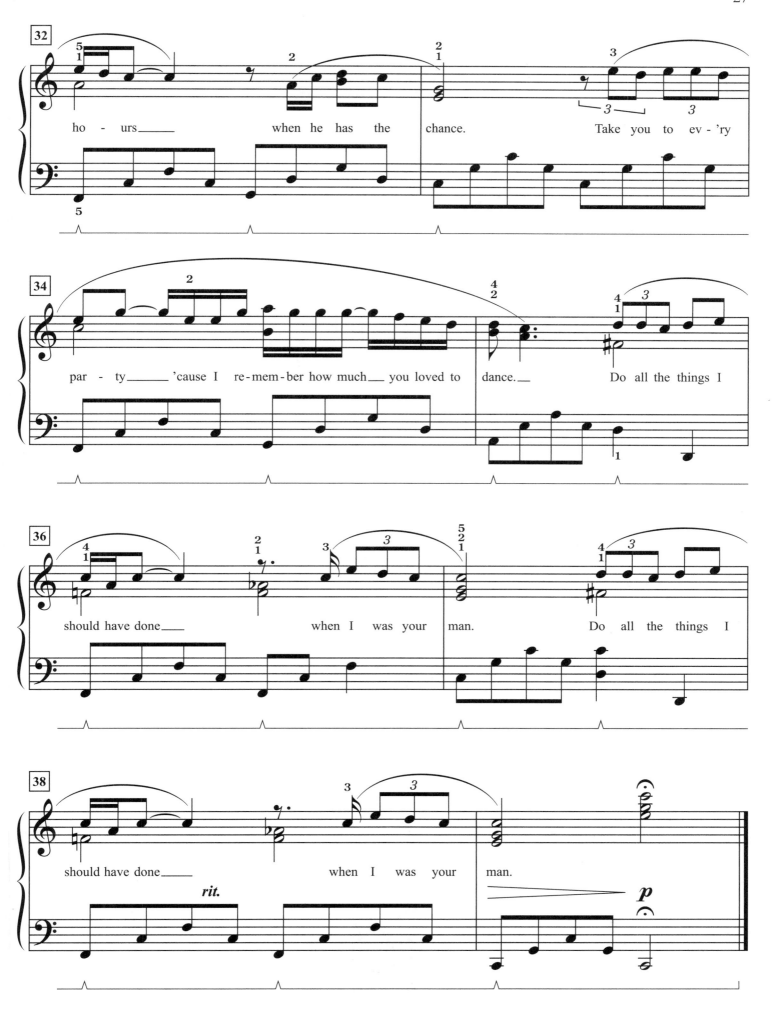